I belong to
THE BEST BOOK CLUB EVER™
This is my book.

My name is

....

Will you please read it to me?

JACK KENT'S Hop, Skip and Jump Book

An Action Word Book

A Random House PICTUREBACK®

JACK KENT'S

Hop, Skip and

Jump Book

An Action Word Book

Random House **New York**

To Kevin and Kim
and Terry Lou

WAKE UP

GET UP

SLEEP

GET UP

BATHE

WIPE

PUT ON

BUTTON

ZIP

BUCKLE

SCRUB

SHAKE

TIE

BRUSH

COMB

PAINT

MODEL

DRAW

CARRY

SWEEP

COPY

COLOR

draw a picture of a

HANG

WRITE

SPILL

CUT

PASTE

LAUGH

PASTE

LIFT

STAGGER

DROP

JUMP

JUMP

LIFT

CARRY

SPLASH

PUSH

SWING

CRY

HIDE

READ

KNIT

HANG

CRAWL

WATCH

SLIDE

CLIMB

SEESAW

BALANCE

RUN

DIG

PULL

PUSH

RIDE

BUMP

CARRY

DIVE

FISH

SWIM

PADDLE

FLOAT

SPLASH

THROW

HIT

CATCH

KICK

CATCH

RUN

JUMP

BOUNCE

THROW

DON'T WALK

CARRY

DRIVE

WASH

PUSH

WAVE

LITTER

KEEP OUR CITY CLEAN

RUN

HOP

FLY

CRAWL

SWIM

RIDE

SWEEP

WEIGH

PUSH

CARRY

STACK

RIDE

TALK

FRUITS AND
VEGETABLES

BAKERY
GOODS

6

COOK

TOAST

CUT

MIX

POUR

EAT

DRINK

KNOCK

OPEN

PLAY

COME IN

GO OUT

SHUT

MELT

PICK UP

THROW

ROLL

SHIVER

SHOVEL

TIE

SLIDE

RIDE

PULL

SKI

HIT

SKATE

FALL

SLIDE

HOP

SKIP

JUMP

SIT

GO TO BED

READ

HUG

KISS

SLEEP

Thank you.